The Adventures of Frog Doctor

The Adventures of Frog Doctor

THOMAS GRAY

ILLUSTRATED BY STEVE LEACH

Xulon Press
2301 Lucien Way #415
Maitland, FL 32751
407.339.4217
www.xulonpress.com

© 2021 by Thomas Gray

Illustrated by Steve Leach

All rights reserved solely by the author. The author guarantees all contents are original and do not infringe upon the legal rights of any other person or work. No part of this book may be reproduced in any form without the permission of the author.

Due to the changing nature of the Internet, if there are any web addresses, links, or URLs included in this manuscript, these may have been altered and may no longer be accessible. The views and opinions shared in this book belong solely to the author and do not necessarily reflect those of the publisher. The publisher therefore disclaims responsibility for the views or opinions expressed within the work.

Unless otherwise indicated, Scripture quotations taken from the King James Version (KJV) – *public domain*.

Paperback ISBN-13: 978-1-66283-648-0
Hard Cover ISBN-13: 978-1-66283-649-7
Ebook ISBN-13: 978-1-66283-650-3

DEDICATION:

To my amazing wife Amy, children, Laurian, Thomas, Dustin, Boone and Sullivan, my dad Lynn (the farmer) and mom Claudette, this book is in remembrance of my wonderful childhood and precious memories growing up.

A special thanks goes out to all the amazing farmers, collectors, and mechanics (just like my dad), who keep these iconic machines alive today, continuing a legacy for our children in generations to come.

THE ADVENTURES OF FROG DOCTOR

There once was this really powerful tractor named Frog Doctor. She was a John Deere tractor and was painted a marvelous shiny green with bright yellow wheels. On the front, she had wheels like a car, but they were close together. On the back, she had giant wheels with really large tires made for digging in the dirt. These tires were as tall as a man, and powering these tires was a really large engine made for pulling.

Frog Doctor was not just any tractor. She was a "Poppin' Johnny." This was the name given to some very special tractors, based on the sound they made..."Puh-choooop, puh-chooop, puh-choop, choop, choop, choop, pop, pop, pop." It was because of these sounds that she was given her name. The farmer's little boy who named her said he thought she was saying, "Frog Doctor, Frog Doctor, Frog Doctor..."

Frog Doctor also had a very unique personality. She was a bit shy and quiet while parked, but she could be loud and noisy whenever it was time to work. She was always friendly and outgoing. Maybe this was because she was the beloved tractor of a farmer in a very small Texas town. The family so adored their mighty machine made of steel. On any given day, the proud tractor could pull as much as a team of twenty-five horses. No matter how much she worked, she never became tired. Perhaps her happy personality was because Frog Doctor had many friends. Her closest pals were the implements she pulled. She pulled plows, trailers, mowers, and grain drills and took very good care of them all. She also loved the farmer's animals, trucks, and other tractors.

Frog Doctor was admired by all the local kids. In return, she loved the kids just as much. Whenever the farmer drove her to town, the kids would run to the edge of the road just to watch Frog Doctor come by. The farmer would let off the throttle, and she would slow down. Frog Doctor would then say, "Puh-choop, pop, pop, pop, pop, choop, choop, choop," and the kids would cheer. Those cheers made Frog Doctor very happy and feel very strong.

BUMBLEBEES

One possible reason that Frog Doctor had such a happy personality was because she had so many adventures. On one such time not long ago, it was a nice spring day. The weather was fine, and there was a comfortable southern breeze. The wind tended to blow a lot in this part of Texas, but on this day, it was much calmer. Those working outdoors always appreciated nice weather, so the farmer decided it was just right outside to do some work with his equipment. Now, some bigger tractors had cabs to protect the farmer, but Frog Doctor only had a seat in the open air. If the weather was bad, the farmer would be exposed to the elements such as rain, snow, heat, or cold. Frog Doctor did not care that she was a basic tractor, though. She did not need a lot of creature comforts such as air conditioning, radios, and such. She was built to work, and that was what she did best.

The farmer attached the mower to Frog Doctor, and they both headed off to the pasture to mow. Frog Doctor was passionate about work, and she was excited to show the farmer how fast she could cut the brush and weeds. Mowing the pasture allowed the grass to thrive. Once the weeds were cut away, the grass could have the water the weeds would have drank. This meant the grass would grow much faster and provide plenty of food for the foraging cattle and horses. Additionally, a freshly-mowed pasture was always nice to look at.

The farmer was delighted with how well his green machine trimmed the weeds. He sighed and thought to himself, *There is no better smell than fresh-cut clover.* After a while, Frog Doctor mowed some very tall grass, but the mower bumped into an old log. Under that log was a bumblebee hive built deep into the ground. This disturbance angered the bumblebees. They flew out of their hole and began to attack Frog Doctor and the farmer. The farmer took off his hat to swat at the bees that were circling his head. He was stung anyway, so he put Frog Doctor in high gear, which allowed them to go much faster. Then, they were able to escape the hostile bees. Frog Doctor was not hurt by the bumblebees and was very happy to help the farmer get away from the angry insects.

The farmer and Frog Doctor continued mowing the remainder of the pasture until it was almost dark. When finished, they drove across the meadow. It had a wonderful fragrance that smelled so good to the farmer. He could also see all of the lines in the grass where Frog Doctor and the mower tires had driven. It almost looked like a circular racetrack, spiraling inward where Frog Doctor had made turn after turn. The pasture was now ready for some rain and the day when the farmer would turn the cows out. What an exciting adventure for Frog Doctor and lesson to be learned by the farmer!

PICKUP TRUCK

On another occasion, after the mowing season had ended, Frog Doctor was parked in the pasture, awaiting her next quest. The spring rain showers began and poured for days. There was so much rain that water began to rise alongside Frog Doctor's large tires. The rain eventually went away, but water was still standing all around her. Meanwhile, the farmer was checking on his cows in the pasture. Wouldn't you know it? His pickup truck became stuck in the mud. The handsome blue pickup truck only had tires made for the highway. They were not made for driving in the mud, so the truck had easily gotten stuck.

The farmer thought and thought about how to get his truck back home. He then remembered Frog Doctor was nearby. The farmer pulled off his boots and waded through the water, which was up to his knees. He climbed aboard his graceful tractor and hit the starter. Frog Doctor's engine started right up. Together, they drove across the swampy pasture. The farmer tied a large chain from Frog Doctor's back to the truck's front bumper. Then, the farmer climbed back up on Frog Doctor and put her in low gear so she could use all her power to pull the truck. He had his youngest son go to steer the pickup truck while Frog Doctor was towing it. Then, the farmer pulled Frog Doctor's throttle handle, giving her gas. This made her mighty engine rev up. As her motor ran faster, you could see the big green flywheels on her sides turn faster as well. You could hear her exhaust pipe bellow out a great, "Puh-choooop, puh-chooop, puh-choop, choop, choop, choop, pop, pop, pop!" Very carefully, the farmer let out on the clutch so his tractor could start moving slowly. Frog Doctor's large back tires began to dig into the mud and take the slack from the chain. She moved forward slowly and began to pull the truck from its deep, muddy ruts. The devoted Frog Doctor briskly pulled the truck through the mud, safely back home. On the way back, the cows and horses came frolicking by, hoping that the farmer had more feed in the back of the truck. Frog Doctor never even broke a sweat and was happy the farmer had asked her for help. From then on, the powerful tractor and the pickup truck were close friends. They often worked together to help the farmer do his work. They would also take care of each other because life on the farm could change at any moment. Pulling the pickup from the mud was one of Frog Doctor's favorite adventures.

BATH TIME

It was now time to get cleaned up, so the farmer took Frog Doctor to town for a bath. Her tires were all coated in mud, and her beautiful yellow wheels had turned brown. She also had mud all over her glossy green paint. Frog Doctor did not have fenders, so the mud would fly off her big tires while she was driving in high gear. Mud clods would shoot into the air and rain down on her and the farmer. What a messy ride! You could even see trails of mud that had come off the tires and onto the roadway. These muddy streaks went from the pasture all the way to the carwash in town.

John Deere tractors are beautiful and well-made machines. They will last a lifetime when properly taken care of. Washing a dirty or muddy tractor is an essential part of maintaining farm equipment. The best farmers always keep their machinery clean. Frog Doctor was well cared for and kept tidy whenever she was not working. She appreciated getting cleaned up, and never argued about taking a bath.

After only a few minutes in the wash, Frog Doctor was clean, and her paint was all shiny again. Taking a bath was one of Frog Doctor's favorite things to do. She liked the spray of the warm, soapy water, and the force of the water would easily spray away the mud and grease on her. First, the farmer would wash all the mud from her tires. Then he would wash the top of Frog Doctor and then her sides and belly. Sometimes he would even wash her engine. Frog Doctor loved having her engine washed. This was because it cleaned away all the old oil and dirt that made her engine run hot. Most importantly, Frog Doctor felt clean and new with a fresh bath.

KIDS

After a good bath, the farmer decided to take Frog Doctor for a spin around the old courthouse. This was where he knew people would stop and look at his awesome tractor. He gave Frog Doctor some throttle, and she perked right up. You could hear her willing engine speed up with her mighty, "Puh-choooop, puh-chooop, puh-choop, choop, choop, choop, pop, pop, pop," and black smoke would billow from her smokestack. On her sides, you could see her flywheels spinning, and they would turn faster whenever her throttle was increased. Sure enough, some kids leaving the general store came outside to see Frog Doctor. They loved watching her big yellow wheels turn and hearing her sounds. One of their favorite things was to watch the tractor do a donut in the wide main street in town. The farmer would turn the steering wheel sharply to the left or right, and he would apply a brake on the same side. Then, Frog Doctor would turn in circles. The kids would laugh and say that she could "turn on a dime." Frog Doctor was so pleased to make the kids laugh.

This day was extra special because some of the kids got to take a ride on Frog Doctor. The farmer knew the kids well and treated them to a ride in his lap. Each would hold on to the steering wheel while the farmer let out on the hand clutch. Frog Doctor would lurch forward gently and take off with no effort at all. The kids would reach up to pull the throttle and make Frog Doctor come to life, and she would sure put on a show for them. When riding on the tractor, some kids wanted to go slow and turn in circles, while others wanted to go fast because her large back tires would make her bounce while going down the street. Taking rides on Frog Doctor was always a thrill for the kids and for the colorful John Deere tractor.

THIRSTY

When play was over, it was time for refreshments. Getting fuel was one of Frog Doctor's favorite things to do. She liked having full fuel tanks. This was because it prevented her tanks from rusting. It also meant she would be ready to go to work. Frog Doctor was equipped with two fuel tanks. One was a small tank that held gasoline while the larger tank held kerosene and other fuels. Frog Doctor was very clever as only a few tractors were made to run on different fuels. Her engine would be started on gasoline. The farmer would then switch a valve after her engine was warmed up, and she would run on the other fuel. The farmer could drive Frog Doctor all day long on a tank of fuel, which pleased him. This made Frog Doctor very happy too. She would gladly show off her power and you could hear her go, "Puh-choooop, puh-chooop, puh-choop, choop, choop, choop, pop, pop, pop."

Tractors are like people in many ways. They hunger for fuel like people hunger for food. Without fuel, Frog Doctor could not do all of the marvelous things that she did. It is also very important to not let tractors run out of fuel. This would mean the farmer would become stranded in the field or pasture. Then, he would have to walk a long distance back home or to the pickup truck. Afterward, he would need to get more fuel. This would require him to carry the fuel across the field to the tractor. Running out of fuel would make the farmer's job very difficult, so he would regularly check to see how much fuel Frog Doctor had in her tanks. Getting fuel is something that tractors cannot do for themselves. Farmers must take extra care to ensure they do not run out. A full tank of fuel always meant a happy tractor; Frog Doctor loved being happy!

HAY TRUCK

It was now time for the big green tractor to go to work. Frog Doctor and the farmer drove back home where there was always something to do. The farmer soon learned that his boys had gotten the big hay truck stuck in the meadow. They had loaded the truck with so much hay that it could not take off in the sand. The truck tires began to spin and dug out deep ruts. It could not go anywhere. The boys had been trying to take the hay to the barn when they'd gotten stuck. The farmer thought at first that he should use a bigger tractor. However, loyal Frog Doctor explained that she was ready and more than able for the task. This time, the mighty green tractor would face one of her greatest challenges. She would be asked to pull a very large truck loaded with hay from a sandy field. So off they went.

The farmer and the boys connected the old truck to Frog Doctor, using its large chain. Then, the farmer put the tractor in low gear and gently let out on the clutch. He revved up her engine using the throttle. Frog Doctor pulled hard on the chain, and her huge back tires began to dig into the sand. The hay truck's bumper strained as the tractor began to pull hard. The truck started to move ever so slightly, and guess what Frog Doctor did? She pulled that massive, heavy truck from the ruts in the sandy field! Everyone was happy and amazed at how strong the green tractor was, and the boys were so happy that they would be able to finish their job. They were very proud of Frog Doctor and so amazed that she had been able to pull the truck out of the sand. The boys even bragged that the farmer's tractor could pull just about anything. Frog Doctor was so thankful that she was able to please the farmer and the boys.

PLANTING TIME

In the early fall that year, it was time to plant the winter pasture. Wheat is a hearty plant that can endure the cold winter and is good for the cattle to graze on. In order to plant the wheat seed, the field needed to be plowed so the seed would go into the ground. The farmer attached a large disk plow to Frog Doctor, and they headed off to the wheat field. The plow was just the right size for his tractor. It had two rows of round disks that were made to cut into the topsoil. Each row was just a little bit wider than Frog Doctor. The plow disks would cut the soil open and flip it over, and the ground would then be just right for planting. The farmer put Frog Doctor in second gear, and he gave her some throttle. Her engine perked up and was ready to pull the plow. You could hear Frog Doctor's engine begin to work as they started moving across the field. She would say, "Puh-choooop, puh-chooop, puh-choop, choop, choop, choop, pop, pop, pop." The plow dug into the dirt, turning it over as the disks moved forward. Frog Doctor and the farmer plowed all day, well into the night. She would use her lights to work after dark. In all, they plowed for three days. Frog Doctor always enjoyed planting season because she was able to spend so much more time with the farmer. He was always impressed by how hard Frog Doctor worked, which pleased him very much.

After plowing, it was time to plant, so a grain drill was hooked up to the tractor. The grain drill was a machine made to be pulled behind Frog Doctor, just like the plow. The drill had two large hoppers that could be filled with grain seed. The seed would fall down several small tubes that ran from the hopper to the ground, and the drill would open the soil just enough so the seeds could fall into the earth and then be covered up. Frog Doctor and the farmer drilled and drilled until the whole field was planted.

The work wasn't done yet, though. Once the seeds started to grow, the wheat would be very hungry, so Frog Doctor was called on to spread fertilizer. She enjoyed spreading the food for the wheat because she knew the plants would love being fed. She also loved using her powerful PTO shaft, which was used to run implements that need rotary power from the back of the tractor. Frog Doctor also enjoyed spreading fertilizer because it was very hard work at first that would get easier as the day wore on. This was because the very large fertilizer hopper would be full in the beginning and would become lighter and easier to pull until all of the fertilizer was gone. Work always made Frog Doctor happy, and she was always willing to please the farmer and help with the crops on the farm.

CATTLE AUCTION

Planting season was over, but it was time to take some cows to the sale. The pasture was muddy because it had been raining, but the farmer needed to load the cows anyway. He knew from past experience that if he used the pickup in the mud, it would likely get stuck. So, he called on Frog Doctor to help. The farmer and his boys had rounded up the cows from the pasture and worked them into the cow lot. They sorted the cows and found the ones that were to be sold. Then it was time to bring in the stock trailer. This time, the farmer's oldest son drove the tractor. Frog Doctor always loved it when the boys would drive her.

The stock trailer was connected to the enthusiastic John Deere. Then off they went across the muddy pasture. Frog Doctor's tires were sinking into the mud, but she was still able to move without any problem. The farmer's son carefully backed the trailer up to the lot so the cows could be loaded. This took several tries because Frog Doctor did not have power steering, which makes turning of the steering wheel easier. He was patient, however, and never gave up. Once the trailer was in position, it was time to load the cows. The farmer and his boys, with their mud boots on, all went into the lot to coax the cows into the trailer. The cows were excited that Frog Doctor was pulling the trailer, so they jumped right in. The farmer quickly closed the gate on the trailer, and his son then climbed back onto the tractor. Together, they drove out of the muddy lot. Once they were back at the barn, the trailer was unhooked from Frog Doctor and then attached to the pickup. The farmer and his boys took the cows to the sale that day. Frog Doctor was grateful to be back at the barn so she could visit with the other cows and the horses. Her tires were very muddy again, but trusty Frog Doctor was sure glad to help the farmer and the boys.

HAYRIDE

Fall was Frog Doctor's favorite time of year. Why? Because it was hayride season. The farmer would drive Frog Doctor up to the small school, where all of the kids would ride on her trailer atop bales of hay. The kids always chose the trailer pulled by Frog Doctor, just so they could hear her say, "Puh-choooop, puh-chooop, puh-choop, choop, choop, choop, pop, pop, pop." The other tractors must have been jealous.

All throughout the day of the hayride, farmers would bring their tractors and hay trailers to town. The kids could see them lining up from school. They became very excited and could not wait until the hayride. After school, the kids who walked home would run toward the tractors to look at them up close. The young people marveled at the powerful machines and would dream of the day when they could drive such a tractor. Sometimes one of the farmers would be there and let the kids climb up on his tractor. They loved it. Frog Doctor was always delighted whenever the kids came over to see her. They would all soon go home and get ready for the hayride that night.

The tractors would leave out just before dark and drive down the old country roads that led from town. The roads were very dark at night because in the country, there are no streetlights. That was not problem for Frog Doctor because she could use her headlights. Near Halloween, the farmhouses were decorated with ghosts and goblins and jack-o-lanterns. The kids would talk, play, and laugh as they made their way through the countryside. The moms and dads were always smiling—perhaps they enjoyed being pulled by Frog Doctor as much as the kids did. It could be scary on those old roads at Halloween, but everyone felt safe being pulled by such a powerful tractor. Frog Doctor enjoyed the scenery almost as much as she did pulling the kids on the trailer.

ON STRIKE

One day soon afterward, Frog Doctor was called on for a different type of challenge. She was asked to join many other tractors in what was known as a farmer's strike. A strike is when workers become unhappy with their labor situation so they stop work to get people's attention. The farmers were going on strike because they were not being paid enough for their crops such as wheat and corn. This meant all of the farmers stopped farming for a short period of time until something could be done about their problem. In order to protest and make a statement to lawmakers about the changes needed, tractors from all over the county were driven to the town square and parked completely around the courthouse. There were tractors everywhere. Frog Doctor was right in the middle of all the action and was happy to help with the cause. After a few weeks, the farmers and tractors' voices were heard by the politicians. The tractors were all able to go home, and the farmers got their price increases. Perhaps all of the tractors would not have made such an impact had it not been for Frog Doctor with her big personality and bright colors. The farmer and his family were very delighted to have their favorite tractor back home.

NEW SEASON

A few days had passed since the strike when a man came to the door of the farmer's house. He had seen Frog Doctor among all the tractors in town and was interested in buying her. At first, the farmer had little desire to let his adored tractor go, so he told the man that he did not want to sell Frog Doctor. While thinking about the man's offer, however, the farmer realized that he actually did need a different type of tractor at that time. He already had a larger tractor but needed a much smaller one that could cultivate the family's garden. The next day, the same man returned and asked the farmer if he had changed his mind about selling Frog Doctor. He even offered the farmer more money. The man knew that John Deere tractors were very reliable and worth the expense to buy. The big question was, would the farmer actually sell his tractor? He thought and thought about it and considered that since he needed a much smaller garden tractor, it would be a good time to trade. No matter what, though, he wanted to make sure that Frog Doctor would have a good home. The farmer relented and agreed to make the sale, only under one condition…that Frog Doctor would be cared for and loved the same way. The man surely agreed. He explained to the farmer that his family would enjoy having Frog Doctor to do their work and be part of their family. The man also had kids who were thrilled and wanted to have their own tractor. He again reassured the farmer that they would take good care of the tractor. So, he paid the farmer and prepared to take Frog Doctor home with him.

    The farmer and his family all gathered together to say goodbye. Frog Doctor reassured the farmer's family that she was happy and eager to join her new family. They waved to Frog Doctor as she rode off into the sunset, driven by a very happy new owner. This was a new season for Frog Doctor. She would be making new friends and doing different things. Frog Doctor was brave and strong through it all. Most of all, she was excited about the opportunity to have many new adventures. As she drove down the old country road, you could hear her a mile away, saying, "Puh-choop, puh-choop, pop, pop, pop, choop, choop, choop, choop, pop, pop, pop!"

AFTERWARD

Frog Doctor was a real Model A John Deere tractor and was used on the Gray family farm located in rural Montague County, Texas. Model A John Deere tractors were very popular with small farms and were the utilitarian backbone of many large farms. John Deere historians state that around 300,000 of these tractors were built from 1934 until 1952. There were as many versions of the tractor as there were uses. Not only were these machines designed to pull implements, but they were also used to power belt-powered machinery. Whenever someone became stuck in the mud or the sand, the Poppin' Johnnys were looked to as a source of liberty from those confines. The name "Frog Doctor" was given to the family's old tractor by the author when he was only three years old because the engine sounded like it was saying, "Frog Doctor." The name stuck, and everyone in the family called the tractor Frog Doctor from then on. The family owned many more tractors over the years, both large and small, one of which was a similar Model A John Deere. The author used this particular tractor, dubbed "Frog Doctor 2," throughout his adolescence. He worked many acres of farmland throughout high school and beyond. A photograph taken of the two was even shared to an audience of 200 people at the author's wedding rehearsal dinner! The old tractors may never die, but they are sorely missed when they go away to new homes.

© 2020 Thomas W. Gray
https://www.theadventuresoffrogdoctor.com
Frog.Doctor@outlook.com

CPSIA information can be obtained
at www.ICGtesting.com
Printed in the USA
JSHW010905170222
23001JS00003B/14

9 781662 836480